WORLD'S MOST
EXTREME

—

By Karen McGhee

Australian
GEOGRAPHIC

WORLD'S MOST EXTREME

World's Most Extreme is published by Australian Geographic, an imprint of Bauer Media Ltd. All images and text are copyright © Bauer Media and may not be reproduced without the written permission of the publishers.

Reprinted in 2019 by

Australian GEOGRAPHIC

54 Park Street, Sydney, NSW 2000
Telephone: (02) 9163 7214
Email: editorial@ausgeo.com.au
www.australiangeographic.com.au
Australian Geographic customer service:
1300 555 176 (local call rate within Australia).
From overseas +61 2 8667 5295

Printed in China by Leo Paper Products

Funds from the sale of this book go to support the Australian Geographic Society, a not-for-profit organisation dedicated to sponsoring conservation and scientific projects, as well as adventures and expeditions.

Editor Lauren Smith
Text Karen McGhee
Book design Katharine McKinnon
Creative director Mike Ellott
Proofreader Erin Mayo
Editor-in-Chief, Australian Geographic Chrissie Goldrick
Managing Director, Australian Geographic Jo Runciman

ALSO IN THIS SERIES:

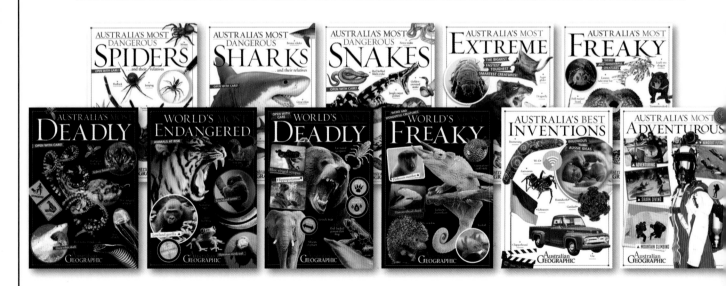

Australian GEOGRAPHIC

WORLD'S MOST
EXTREME

CONTENTS

MASSIVE MOLARS

GIANT PANDA

Although giant pandas have a largely vegetarian diet and eat mostly bamboo, they are actually classified scientifically as carnivores, which are the meat-eating animals. As a result of their bamboo-chomping lifestyle, pandas have evolved the biggest molar teeth of any carnivore. These, along with their strong jaws, allow them to crush hard bamboo stems as big as 4cm wide.

FAST FACT

Constant eaters
Because bamboo has such low nutrient levels, adult pandas need to each eat about 20kg a day. That can take them as long as 16 hours to eat.

LARGEST AMPHIBIAN

CHINESE GIANT SALAMANDER

This huge relative of frogs and toads can grow to a length of almost 1.8m. But, sadly, there are very few left now and they are rarely seen at that size.

EXTINCTION THREAT

The Chinese giant salamander is critically endangered due partly to hunting for use in traditional Chinese medicine.

LARGEST SPIDER

30cm long

GIANT HUNTSMAN SPIDER

The famous goliath birdeater might be the largest spider when measured by weight, but the giant huntsman spider takes the prize when it comes to sheer size. This huntsman was only discovered in 2001, in a cave in the South East Asian country of Laos, which lies north of Thailand. If this slender spider species sat on a dinner plate its legs would stretch right across. No other spider has such a long leg span – up to 30cm.

MOST EYES

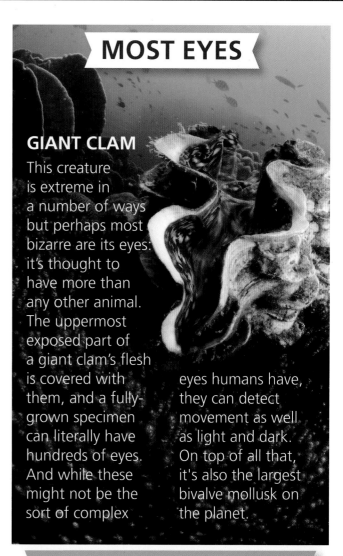

GIANT CLAM

This creature is extreme in a number of ways but perhaps most bizarre are its eyes: it's thought to have more than any other animal. The uppermost exposed part of a giant clam's flesh is covered with them, and a fully-grown specimen can literally have hundreds of eyes. And while these might not be the sort of complex eyes humans have, they can detect movement as well as light and dark. On top of all that, it's also the largest bivalve mollusk on the planet.

SMALLEST MAMMAL

BUMBLEBEE BAT

This tiny furred creature weighs less than some insects. In fact, this species is about as small as a mammal can be, as being warm-blooded at this tiny size requires a huge amount of energy. These bats grow no bigger than two grams, with a head and body length of just 29–33mm.

FACT BOX — SMALL SHREWS

The bumblebee bat is the smallest mammal by absolute size, but the very slightly bigger Etruscan shrew happens to weigh a tiny bit less. It's average weight is 1.8g.

WEIRDEST TUSKS

NORTH SULAWESI BABIRUSA

It's well-known that the tusks on elephants and rhinos and the antlers of deer and antelope are weapons, used against predators and to spar against males of the same species.

But no one is quite sure about the purpose of the tusks on a male babirusa, though they are thought to potentially protect their eyes. These extraordinary features are actually upper canine teeth that grow out from the jaw and through the nose to curve back towards the forehead. The lower canines of a male babirusa are also sharp and protruding. There are four babirusa species, all of which are found in Indonesia. The North Sulawesi species is the largest and can grow tusks to a length of more than 40cm, which eventually repenetrate the skull.

FACT BOX — USELESS WEAPONS

Bubirusa tusks are so brittle that they break off easily, making them useless as weapons or for any other purpose other than display.

LONGEST GESTATION PERIOD

ASIAN ELEPHANT

All elephant species have an exceptionally long gestation period (the full length of an average pregnancy). Elephant mums are pregnant for 20.5 to 22 months, which is nearly two years and longer than any other animal. That's more than twice as long as the human gestation period of 9 months. Despite being smaller than its African relatives, the average Asian elephant's gestation period is just a little bit longer, ahead by a few days.

WIDEST CRAB

4m long

JAPANESE SPIDER CRAB

When it comes to width, no crab is bigger than the Japanese spider crab, which is found mostly in waters up to 600m deep in the Pacific Ocean off the coast of Japan. Although the carapace (the shell covering the main body) of these crabs is usually no longer than about 37cm, the leg span of adults can be massive – as wide as 4m, which is wider than a bus! The Japanese spider crab can weigh up to 20kg.

AMAZING POWERS OF REGENERATION

ZEBRAFISH

Scientists are looking to the small freshwater zebrafish from the Himalayas to learn how to fix broken hearts. Zebrafish are vertebrates, with a heart a lot like ours. But they have a very special and unique capability for regeneration. When a zebrafish heart is wounded, the site is quickly sealed off by a clot and the surrounding heart muscle slowly grows over it. Soon the heart is almost as good as new and pumping just as strongly as ever.

FASTEST FISH

BLACK MARLIN

Like many animal records, not everyone agrees on the species that takes this title. Regularly the Indo-Pacific sailfish is at the top of the fastest fish list, as it's been recorded slicing through the tropical waters of the Indian and Pacific oceans at speeds of more than 110km/h in short bursts. More recently, however, another fish has laid claim to the title of fastest fish. Based on the rate at which hooked black marlins unwind fishing line from a reel, scientists have estimated that this fish can reach a top speed of 129km/h.

LONGEST REPTILE

RETICULATED PYTHON

South East Asia's reticulated python doesn't get as heavy as South America's anaconda, but it certainly seems to grow longer. There have been many reports of individuals longer than 6m and the longest officially documented individual was 7.67m. In 2016 a specimen was caught on the Malaysian island of Penang that was estimated to be 8m long and weigh 250kg.

8m long

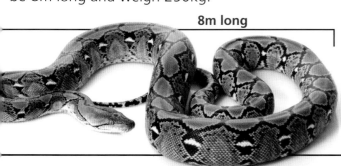

FASTEST PUNCH AND AMAZING EYESIGHT

FAST FACT

Captive vandals
Peacock mantis shrimp have been known to punch and break the glass walls of tanks when kept in captivity.

PEACOCK MANTIS SHRIMP

The peacock mantis shrimp is a stunning-looking creature that has two extreme claims to fame. Firstly, this colourful crustacean has a dark side: it likes to punch and it does so at a startling 80km/h – faster than has been recorded for any other animal. It has two front claws specially adapted for punching through the tough shells of molluscs to reach the soft tissue inside, which it eats. The other astounding feature of peacock mantis shrimps is their eyesight. They have highly specialised eyes that can see colour better than most animals, including us. Even more impressive is that they can also detect several different types of light, including infrared and ultraviolet light and even a type of polarised light that no other animal is known to be able to detect.

EUROPE

FAST FACT

Head space
The sperm whale has another extreme feature: it has an 8kg brain, the largest of any animal that has ever lived.

LOUDEST ANIMAL

SPERM WHALE

The animal kingdom is full of squawking, screeching, rumbling loud-mouths, but the loudest of them all is the sperm whale. These huge deep-ocean creatures appear to be able to communicate by producing clicking noises, the loudest of which have been measured at 230 **decibels** (dB). To give you an idea of how loud this is, a jet airplane taking off is about 165dB. Fortunately, sperm whale clicks are quick (no more than 30 milliseconds) but they can be heard by another sperm whale more than 16km away.

HIGH-DENSITY DWELLER

JUMPING APPARATUS

Most springtail species have a jumping organ called a furcula attached to their abdomens.

SPRINGTAILS

Ever feel that you're not alone? Chances are you never have been. The world is crawling with life, and we're not just talking bacteria or other microscopic flora and fauna. Among the most abundant creatures in the world are insect-like creatures called springtails. With most between 2–6mm long, many different types are visible to the naked eye, if you look out for them. Springtails live in high humidity environments, where they feed on substances such as mould, bacteria and decaying plant matter. Scientists estimate their numbers to be as high as 100,000 per cubic metre, even in places where they are living side-by-side with people.

MOST BRAIN CELLS

LONG-FINNED PILOT WHALE

The neocortex is a part of the brain that is particularly well-developed in humans. Neuroscientists had always assumed we had more nerve cells in the neocortex than any other species. They got a shock in 2014 when a study of the brains of long-finned pilot whales in the North Atlantic found that this species has more brain cells in the neocortex than any other species ever studied, and almost twice as many neurons in this part of the brain as humans. Scientists are still wrestling with what this might mean about the intelligence of pilot whales.

LARGEST INVERTEBRATE

GIANT SQUID

There's no doubt the giant squid is certainly the largest invertebrate alive today, but no one is quite sure just *how* big it gets. Suspected to be the cause of many sea monster myths, this enormous mollusc species is rarely seen as it lives at great depths in the Atlantic Ocean where it feeds on deep-sea fishes and squid. But there have been reports of 18m-long specimens that have washed up on beaches.

FOUR-HEARTED FISH

HAGFISH

Hagfish are ancient fish with four hearts, part of a primitive system that circulates blood around their bodies. One heart acts as the main pump while the other three help out. Another extreme hagfish feature is how they eat: they burrow deep into the dead bodies of other animals to eat their rotting flesh from the inside out. Then there's their response to **predators**. When something tries to grab them they produce such huge quantities of slime that they're impossible to get hold of.

EUROPE

ARCTIC TERN

These small birds embark on a huge annual **migration** that takes them around the planet and back, further than any other bird. Every year they fly from breeding grounds in the Arctic to the other end of the world to spend the southern hemisphere summer feeding on small fish and crustaceans in waters off Antarctica and then fly back again.

It's a return journey that can take them, on average, across more than 70,000km. They're long-lived birds and many will complete this return trip more than 20 times during their lifetime.

FAST FACT

Precision returners
Most Arctic terns return to breed at the same place, and usually in the same colony, where they themselves hatched.

ONLY COLOUR CHANGING DOG

ARCTIC FOX

The Arctic fox is the only member of the dog family that changes its coat colour as the weather warms. It's white for much of the year when its habitat is also shrouded in white snow, and it needs to be **camouflaged** so that it can sneak up on its prey. But as the snow and ice melts in spring and summer and the Arctic tundra is transformed by darker tones, the head, legs, tail and back of the Arctic fox turn brown while its sides and underbelly take on lighter tones.

LONGEST-LIVING VERTEBRATE

GREENLAND SHARK

Found mostly in deep waters off the North Atlantic and Arctic oceans, the Greenland shark is thought to live longer than any other vertebrate. By counting layers of proteins in the lens of the eyes of female sharks caught in nets, scientists estimated that this huge fish can live for more than 400 years. It's known that female Greenland sharks can't reproduce until after they reach 4m in length, which means they must be about 150 years old before they produce their first young.

LONGEST ANIMAL

55m long

BOOTLACE WORM

The bootlace worm, a marine invertebrate found in sediment along the British coast, could make the cut as the world's longest animal. Specimens are often found between 5–15m long, but can reach much greater lengths with reports of individuals that can be stretched out to 55m, longer than any other creature – even the blue whale.

DEEPEST AND LONGEST DIVER

CUVIER'S BEAKED WHALE

No other mammal dives deeper or longer than Cuvier's beaked whale. Using **satellite tags** to track whales off the Californian coast, scientists have recorded adult individuals of this species diving to depths of almost 3km during dives of longer than two hours. Exactly how these whales manage to navigate and withstand the immense pressure at these sorts of depths is not yet fully understood. But they're thought to have collapsible rib cages to reduce air pockets that would make them buoyant as they dived.

ONLY ANIMAL TO LIVE FOREVER

IMMORTAL JELLYFISH

Life for this jellyfish species begins, as it does for all jellyfish, as a larva that swims about in the **plankton**. Unlike most other jellyfish, however, this larvae ultimately settles down onto the sea floor to develop into a colony of attached creatures known as polyps. From these, free-swimming jellyfish bud off and reach adulthood in a matter of weeks and at a size of less than half a centimeter. If, however, these are threatened or injured in any way they revert back to the polyp stage and create a new colony from which new adults are budded. This cycle can go on indefinitely. It's as if the jellyfish can simply 'press a reset button' every time life gets tough.

MOST DISGUSTING BIRD

NORTHERN FULMAR

Fulmar chicks are as fluffy and cute as any other baby bird, but they're certainly not as defenceless. Their response to a potential threat or predator is to vomit up a vile orange-coloured concoction from deep in their gut, which they can shoot up to 1.8m. This acts a deterrent not only because it smells disgustingly of rotten fish but also because it is so sticky that it's almost impossible to remove, even with repeated scrubbing.

AFRICA

Decision-making
Most animals act out of instinct, but chimpanzees can alter their behaviour and make decisions based on what they see.

SMARTEST ANIMAL

CHIMPANZEE

There are many different ways to measure intelligence and different animals are smart in different ways. But scientists continue to be astounded by the intellect of the chimpanzee – one of the species most closely related to humans. Dutch primatologist Fras de Waal named a chimp called Ayumu as number one on his list of smart animals because he outperformed humans on a memory test. They are also known to learn words, to use tools and play with objects.

MOST ABUNDANT BIRD

RED-BILLED QUELEA

This small brown finch lives on Africa's **savannah** grasslands and doesn't look like anything extraordinary – in fact it looks a lot like a common sparrow. But it likes hanging with other red-billed queleas so much that it can form super-colonies of up to 30 million birds. Each quelea can eat half its bodyweight in grain per day, which is about 10g of grain, meaning that a flock of two million birds can devour up to 20 tonnes of grain in a single day. It's for this reason that, as well as being the world's most abundant bird, the red-billed quelea has another claim-to-fame – one of Africa's most hated birds! Its huge flocks are able to decimate entire fields of crops within hours.

FAST FACT

Flying pests
The estimated breeding population of red-billed queleas is 1.5 billion birds.

LARGEST SNAIL

AFRICAN GIANT SNAIL

No other slug or snail gets bigger than this massive mollusc. The largest African giant snail ever recorded was 39.3cm long, from the end of its out-stretched tail to the tip of its snout – longer than a school ruler. It weighed 900g and had a 27.3cm-long shell.

These squidgy invertebrates (distant relatives of octopuses and squids) are vegetarians; munching on plant matter, living or dead, at night in their forest habitat. From their West African home, these snails have spread worldwide.

MASTER INVADER

The African giant snail is one of the top 100 most invasive species in the world.

900g

LARGEST BIRD EGG

2.589kg
Biggest egg ever recorded

Of all living birds, the common ostrich lays the largest eggs and the biggest one ever recorded was laid in 2008 by a farmed ostrich. It weighed a massive 2.589kg. Within a herd, all the eggs will be grouped together in one nest, and laid on by the dominant female and male of the herd.

FACT BOX **BIG BIRDS**

Common ostriches can grow 2.7m tall and weigh up to 160kg.

AFRICA

AFRICAN BUSH ELEPHANT

When it comes to records for heaviest living land animals, the surviving species of elephant top the list. The African bush elephant comes first with males, according to some estimates, capable of reaching weights of more than 7 tonnes. African forest elephants and Asian elephants can reach more than 5 tonnes – enough to put them second and third in the heaviest animal stakes. Elephants are vegetarians, eating mostly roots, grass, fruits and bark. Adult elephants have been known to eat more than 130kg of this sort of plant material every day.

FAST FACT

Massive movers
Despite their huge size, elephants can run at up to 25km/h, and maybe even faster!

7 tonnes

BIGGEST HERD

SPRINGBOK

When these antelopes were migrating across the western plains of southern Africa they formed the largest known herds of any animals on Earth. These huge aggregations could be 145km long and contained tens of millions of individual springbok. In the last 120 years though, the human impacts of hunting, urbanisation, farming and development have severely impact their numbers and prevented their migration.

FACT BOX — TEAM UP

One of the main reasons animals form herds is so they can work together to keep watch and warn each other about any approaching predators.

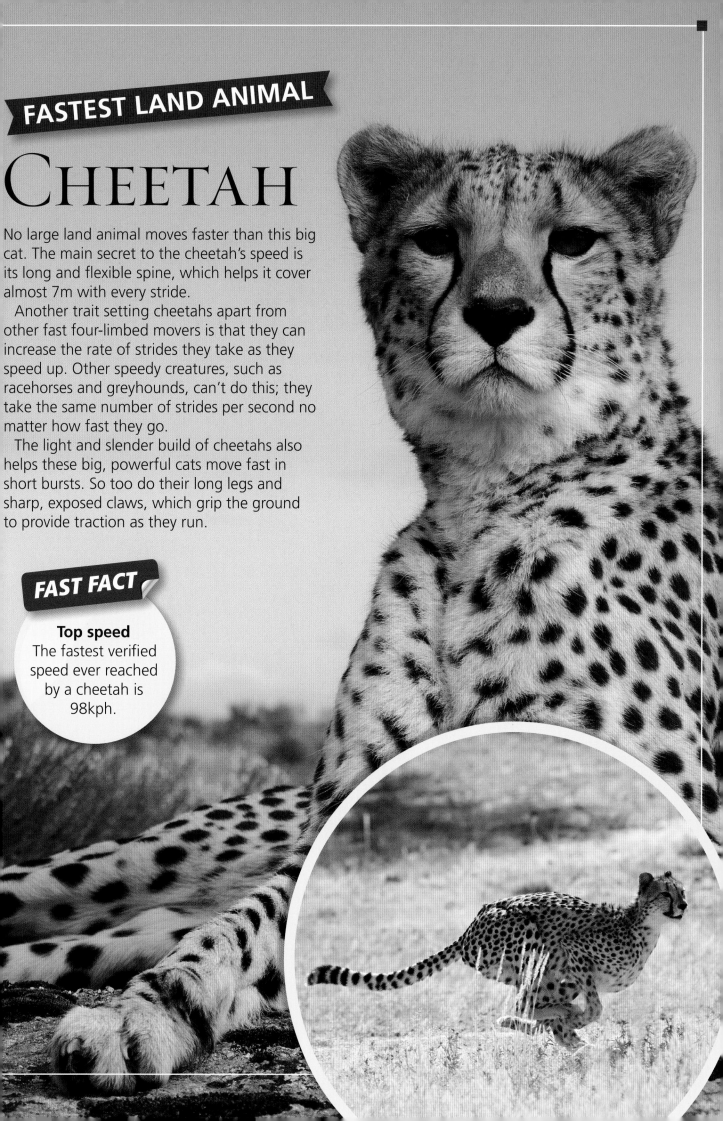

CHEETAH

No large land animal moves faster than this big cat. The main secret to the cheetah's speed is its long and flexible spine, which helps it cover almost 7m with every stride.

Another trait setting cheetahs apart from other fast four-limbed movers is that they can increase the rate of strides they take as they speed up. Other speedy creatures, such as racehorses and greyhounds, can't do this; they take the same number of strides per second no matter how fast they go.

The light and slender build of cheetahs also helps these big, powerful cats move fast in short bursts. So too do their long legs and sharp, exposed claws, which grip the ground to provide traction as they run.

FAST FACT

Top speed
The fastest verified speed ever reached by a cheetah is 98kph.

AFRICA

GIRAFFE

Male giraffes can grow to a height of 5.5m, well over 2m more than the next tallest animal, the African elephant. An adult giraffe's neck alone is 1.8m long and its legs are about the same.

Why are giraffes so tall? One obvious theory is that extreme height gives them an advantage foraging for food in treetops, which shorter animals can't reach from the ground. A more recent theory is that giraffes evolved long necks in males as a secondary sexual characteristic. That means long necks give males a way of competing for mates. You can see just how they do that in a method of fighting called "necking", during which males violently swing their necks around at each other.

5.5m tall

FAST FACT

Perfect name
A group of a giraffes is called a tower.

HIGHEST MAMMAL JUMPER

KLIPSPRINGER

These African antelopes are just 60cm tall at the shoulder but can jump to a height of 15m, more than 12 times taller than they are. That makes them the highest jumper of all mammals when compared to body size. This extraordinary capability makes it hard for potential predators, such as leopards, hyenas and baboons, to grab them.

NAME-CALLING

In Swahili, an African language, Klipspringer means "goat of the rocks".

LARGEST FROG

GOLIATH FROG

Most of the world's frog species are small enough to fit neatly on the palm of a human hand. But that's certainly not the case for the goliath frog, which can reach the proportions of a newborn human baby – more than 3kg in weight and longer than 30cm.

FAST FACT

No croak
African goliath frogs have no vocal sac and so don't call for mates as other frogs do.

WITHSTANDS GREAT HEAT

FAST FORAGERS

Sahara Desert ants brave hot desert conditions to scavenge for the carcasses of invertebrates, such as spiders and insects.

SAHARA DESERT ANT

This tiny insect is one of the most heat-tolerant creatures in the world. It's one of a few creatures able to withstand the searing midday heat of the Sahara Desert, which is the hottest **terrestrial** habitat on the entire planet. It leaves its sandy burrow at the hottest time of the day, when the surface temperature can reach 70°C, but the ant must keep its body below the critical maximum temperature of 55.1°C to survive.

EMPEROR PENGUIN

This bird breeds in the coldest place on Earth – Antarctica in winter. There, on the open ice, male emperor penguins huddle together, each with a single egg held up off the ground on their feet and kept warm in a feathered belly pouch. Standing like this, they'll resolutely face months of the worst winter conditions that occur anywhere, including wind chills as low as -60°C and 200kph blizzards. Male emperor penguins also won't feed during that entire time, until their partners return from foraging to relieve them of their egg-incubating duties.

FAST FACT

Penguin stats
Emperors, the largest of the world's 17 penguin species, reach a height of 1.15m and up to 45kg in weight.

WEIRDEST DEFENCE

SEA CUCUMBERS

Sea cucumbers, which are relatives of starfish and sea urchins, have one of the most extreme forms of defence against predators. When threatened, these cylinder-shaped creatures can expel their internal organs – particularly their guts – sending them out through either their mouths or the other end, depending on the species. It's a behaviour known as evisceration. It's used to scare off the crabs and fish that prey on sea cucumbers. The organs regenerate inside the sea cucumbers within five weeks, and these animals appear to suffer no long-term ill effects.

BIGGEST JELLYFISH

LION'S MANE JELLYFISH

This is not only the jellyfish longest known to science but also a contender for the longest animal on Earth. The biggest known specimen was found dead washed up on a beach. It had a 2.3m-wide bell and 37m-long tentacles, exceeding the 30m reached by blue whales but possibly not as long as the saltwater bootlace worm.

HUMAN IMPACT · FACT BOX

These jellyfish have a painful sting that can cause blisters and muscular cramps and may affect respiratory and heart function. Despite that, stings are not usually fatal for people.

BIGGEST ANIMAL EVER

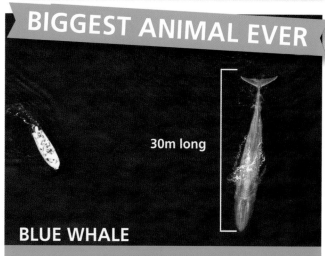

30m long

BLUE WHALE

It's thought that no other animal that's ever lived on Earth has achieved the size of the blue whale, not even the biggest dinosaurs. The largest blue whale on record weighed almost 200 tonnes and was more than 30m long. They might be the biggest creatures, but blue whales prey only on tiny crustaceans called krill which they strain from polar waters. They eat up to four tonnes of krill a day.

LARGEST EGG FOR BODY SIZE

KIWIS

The kiwi, a flightless bird found only on the Pacific Island nation of New Zealand, produces the largest egg of any bird in relation to the mother's body size. These eggs are six times bigger than would be expected for a bird the size of a kiwi, and take up about 25 per cent of the mother's body. While the ostrich produces the largest egg of any bird, it only takes up about 2 per cent of its mother's body.

OCEANIA

BIGGEST SHARK

WHALE SHARK

The whale shark, which migrates annually to feed on tiny plankton in waters off the coast of Western Australia, is the world's largest fish. Adults can reach a length of more than 10m and a weight of almost 19 tonnes. These sharks also have the thickest skin of any animal – up to 14cm thick. This is also extremely tough, being covered in tiny tooth-like scales known as dermal denticles. Not only does whale-shark skin help protect these fish from pretty much any potential predator, it also helps reduce drag in the water as they swim.

LARGEST BUTTERFLY

30cm long

QUEEN ALEXANDRA'S BIRDWING

The largest butterflies in the world are female Queen Alexandra's birdwings. They have a wingspan of almost 30cm. The species is extremely sexual dimorphic, meaning that males and females look very different: the males are smaller than the females and have such different physical markings that they look like different species. These stunning insects are found only in coastal rainforests in eastern Papua New Guinea and are endangered due to destruction of their habitat to make way for palm oil plantations.

REPTILE WITH A THIRD EYE

TUATARA

Despite their appearance, these native New Zealand creatures are not lizards. They are the only surviving members of the *Rhynchocephalia*, an ancient group that flourished as long as 200 million years ago. All but the tuatara went extinct around 60 million years ago. Tuataras have a third eye, known as a parietal eye. It's located on the top of the head, though by the time the tuatara reaches four months old it's usually covered in skin and scales. It isn't used for vision, but for regulating temperature and sleep patterns.

FASTEST LIZARD

CENTRAL BEARDED DRAGON

When it comes to the world's fastest lizard, there are at least two contenders. One is the black spiny-tailed iguana of South and Central America, which has officially been clocked running at almost 35kph. But Australia's central bearded dragon, which rises up on its hind legs when threatened by a predator and races across the landscape at what's estimated to be around 40km/h, could prove to be more worthy of the 'world's fastest lizard' title.

FASTEST BIRD

PEREGRINE FALCON

During its hunting dives the peregrine falcon can reach more than 320km/h as it plummets from great heights to swoop in and grab or stun prey. These streamlined, powerfully built birds-of-prey hunt other birds as well as mammals, such as rabbits. When chasing other birds, peregrine falcons can also fly at great speeds, although not quite as fast as they achieve when plummeting under gravity.

DEADLIEST ANT

BULLDOG ANT

There are about 90 species in the Australian ant genus *Myrmecia*, which are most commonly referred to as bull ants. Some of these are known to be potentially harmful to humans. *Myrmecia* have caused more human deaths than any other ants. All together at least six people in Australia have died from **anaphylaxis** – an extreme allergic reaction – after being bitten by *Myrmecia* ants. Five of these have occurred on the Australian island of Tasmania, where at least one study has shown that up to 3 per cent of the population is allergic to the venom of the ants. That's twice the level of people allergic to the venom of European honeybees.

HEAVIEST CRAB

17kg

TASMANIAN GIANT CRAB

This crustacean is found in the cold, deep ocean waters off southern Australia. Males grow to weights of more than 17kg, making it the world's heaviest crab, although the largest by leg span is the Japanese spider crab. The shells of the largest specimens of Tasmanian giant crabs are up to 46cm wide.

FACT BOX **SLOW BREEDERS**

Tasmanian giant crabs can only mate when they moult, which is when they shed their shells to grow. In adult females this only happens about every nine years.

BEST SENSE OF SMELL

AMERICAN BLACK BEAR

Few animals can challenge this native North American bear's ability to detect smells. Its nose looks large from the outside but what truly sets this creature apart are the folds of tissue lining it. Constantly kept moist, this tissue (known as the nasal mucosa) covers an area 100 times bigger than it does in our human nose. Black bears are estimated to be have a sense of smell at least seven times better than the bloodhound, a breed of dog renowned for its ability to sniff things out.

FAST FACT

Knowing noses
The black bear's sense of smell allows it to detect a smell at least 2km away. Some scientists think they may even be able to detect smells more than 30km away.

NOT-SO-SPEEDY SLUG

BANANA SLUGS

Slugs and snails have reputations as slow movers…extremely slow movers! And banana slugs seem to be among the slowest. While the average garden snail moves at a rate of about 78cm per minute, these bright-yellow, North American slugs move at, well, considerably less than a snail's pace – at 17cm per minute.

LONG LIVES

Banana slugs can live for as long as seven years.

UV VISION

REINDEER

The eyes of most mammals can only detect light in the visible part of the spectrum. But reindeers have a unique visual adaptation that means they are the only mammals that can also see ultraviolet (UV) light. This is believed to be an adaptation to the Arctic environment where they live, as snow and ice reflect a lot of UV light. In contrast lichen, which is eaten by reindeer, and the bodies of predators absorb UV light. And so being able to see UV light makes it much easier for reindeer to locate their food and avoid predators such as wolves.

SHORTEST LIFE SPAN

MAYFLY

All mayflies have short adult lives but females of the uncommon *Dolania americana* species take it to the extreme. They live as adults for just five minutes, enough time to mate and lay eggs. After hatching, they burrow into riverbeds where they feed on the larvae of small insects. After about a year as nymphs, males and females emerge and transform into winged adults. Within a few short minutes the next generation is created and the cycle begins again.

HASTY HEARTBEATS

AMERICAN PYGMY SHREW

This is North America's smallest mammal by weight. Adults grow to just 2–4g and maintaining body heat at this tiny size is a constant challenge. It's why these shrews have one of the fastest heartbeats of any mammal (1200 beats per minute). To sustain such a rapid rate they need to eat three times their body weight every day and so their life is spent almost constantly foraging for food such as beetles, spiders and other small invertebrates. They only ever sleep for a few minutes at a time.

NORTH AMERICA

STRIPED SKUNK

There are a few animals that use extreme smell as a form of self-defence and skunks are perhaps the best known. These black-and-white mammals don't even try to outrun a threat: instead they simply turn their backside at a would-be attacker and spray a noxious substance from large anal glands near the base of the tail. They can spray this oily, hard-to-remove substance out across a distance of three metres and most predators would run away rather than take on a skunk.

FAST FACT

Shared aroma
The chemicals that make skunk spray smell so bad, which are known as thiols, are also found in rotting flesh and faeces.

STINKIEST MAMMAL

LONG LIFECYCLES

PERIODIC CICADA

Nearly all cicadas spend some of their life underground as juveniles, emerging from the ground to experience a short life as adults. Periodic cicadas are remarkable for their synchronicity (each generation of cicadas emerges at once), and for their lifespan – they'll spend 13 or 17 years underground as nymphs before emerging! They live for four to six weeks as adults. Within two months, they'll be gone and new cicada eggs will have been laid.

MOST ABUNDANT VERTEBRATES

BRISTLEMOUTHS

These tiny **bioluminescent** fish don't just occur in the waters off North America, but in deep water right throughout the world's temperate ocean habitats. Scientists believe that one bristlemouth **genus** (*Cyclothone*) is the most abundant of any on Earth. There are thought to be more individual *Cyclothone* bristlemouths than any other vertebrate – hundreds of trillions of them and possibly even quadrillions (which is thousands of trillions).

SLOWEST FLYING BIRD

AMERICAN WOODCOCK

American woodcocks fly at a respectable rate of 26–45km/h when they migrate. But during an elaborate aerial courtship 'dance' performed by males to attract mates, these birds can fly so slowly that they almost stall in mid-air. During these flights the males will fly as slow as 8km/h, the slowest flying speed recorded for a bird. Each male woodcock has a few preferred sites where he performs his courtship flights and also sings to impress prospective mates.

TEXAS LONGHORN

Sometimes animals live up to their names perfectly! And that's exactly the case with this North American breed of cattle – the Texas longhorn. The average width of the horns on bulls in this breed is 1.8m from tip to tip and can be even longer in some steers and extraordinary cows. But there's one particular steer that makes the average horn length seem short. Known by the grand name of Lazy J's Bluegrass, in 2015, he was acknowledged as the longhorn with the largest horn spread – a massive 2.978m wide.

CAN SURVIVE BEING FROZEN

WOOD FROG

Very few animals can be frozen and not die, and the wood frog is one of them. During the long Alaskan winters it buries itself in the ground and enters a deep state of **hibernation**. It doesn't breathe, its heartbeat stops and most of the water in its body turns to ice. At the height of winter its body temperature hovers between -10°C and -60°C. As spring arrives and it thaws out, bodily functions return and it hops off to begin breeding as soon as possible.

LOWEST BODY TEMPERATURE IN AN ANIMAL

ARCTIC GROUND SQUIRREL

Alaska's Arctic ground squirrel has many adaptations that allow it to survive the harsh Arctic environment but hibernating, which it does for up to 8 months of every year, is its most effective response. Researchers have discovered that these squirrels drop their body temperature down to the lowest-ever recorded for a mammal – to below freezing. This slows the squirrel's **metabolism** down, which helps it to conserve energy so that it can survive its long hibernation, when it doesn't feed or drink.

FACT BOX **MASSIVE LOSS**

The Arctic ground squirrel loses about half of its body weight during the eight months it hibernates.

BIG-BEAKED BIRDS

FAST FACT

Fruit-eaters
Toco toucans are mostly frugivores: they eat mainly fruits that they pick from the forest canopy.

TOCO TOUCAN

This is the largest toucan species and it has the biggest beak for its body size of any bird; it's one-twentieth of the toucan's total weight and one-third its total length. Bright but clever colouration ensures these birds are perfectly camouflaged in their homes in Brazil's forest and savannahs. But then they seem to go and blow their cover with some of the most varied and noisy vocalisations of any birds. They produce a persistent rattle that sounds like they are having an ongoing conversation. And they create deep croaks that they also repeat incessantly.

SUPERSTRENGTH

HERCULES BEETLE

As its common name suggests, this small creature, which is large for an insect, has extraordinary strength. It's found in the jungles of South America and is famously able to lift objects 850 times its own bodyweight. That would be like a human weightlifter hoisting 65 tonnes above his head! The other weird feature of these beetles is the enormous pincers that protrude from the heads of males. They look like massive horns, which is why the group this insect belongs to is known as the rhinoceros beetles.

LONGEST MAMMAL TONGUE

TUBE-LIPPED NECTAR BAT

The 8.5cm-long tongue of this bat stretches one-and-a-half-times its body length. In fact, when compared to the bat's overall body size, it's longer than the tongue of any other mammal. It's only beaten by the ridiculously long tongues of chameleons, a group of lizards found mostly on the African island of Madagascar.

BIGGEST SNAKE

GREEN ANACONDA

Two species vie for the title of biggest snake. The reticulated python is likely to be the longest but when it comes to sheer bulk, snakes don't get any heavier than a fully grown green anaconda. The largest anaconda ever to be verified weighed 97.2kg and was 5.2m long. There are, however, reports of a specimen of more than 8.5m long, measuring 30cm around its belly and estimated to have weighed more than 220kg.

SOUTH AMERICA

LARGEST RODENT

CAPYBARA

At more than a metre in length and reaching weights of more than 60kg, capybaras are many times larger than their close relative, the guinea pig. Capybaras are widespread in lowland habitats of South America near wetlands, swamps and flooded grasslands where they live partially aquatic lives.

WATER BABIES

Capybaras are strong swimmers that can remain submerged underwater for up to five minutes at a time. They also mate in water.

SMALLEST BIRD

BEE HUMMINGBIRD

This tiny little creature is the world's smallest bird. It reaches a maximum bodyweight of less than 2g and a length of less than 6cm. Like other hummingbirds it feeds mainly on nectar that it takes from a variety of flower species as it hovers with great precision at the entrances to blooms. The bee hummingbird will also, however, eat insects.

As with other tiny mammals, hummingbirds need a fast metabolism to remain active at such a small physical size. They need to eat up to half their bodyweight in food every day and eight times their bodyweight in water.

FAST FACT

Reverse fliers
Hummingbirds are the only birds capable of controlled backwards flight; a handy skill for moving back out of blooms when feeding.

GOLDEN POISON DART FROG

We've all heard of deadly snakes, venomous spiders and jellyfish that can kill you with their stings. But who'd have thought a tiny frog would be up there among the world's most toxic creatures? Adult golden poison dart frogs grow no longer than 5cm and yet each contains enough poison in its skin to kill up to 10 adult humans. Indigenous people living in South America's forests have for centuries been applying poison from this frog and others like it to the sharp tips of darts used for hunting.

FAST FACT

Frog benefit
Medical researchers have developed a synthetic version of a compound called batrachotoxin found in poison dart frog skin that they hope to develop as a powerful painkiller for people.

SOUTH AMERICA

SLEEPIEST ANIMALS

LARGE HAIRY ARMADILLO

When it comes to sleepy animals, this species is up there with the best. Other big sleepers, such as Australia's koalas and South America's sloths, tend to survive on food that's very low in nutritional value, so they don't have the energy to do much else beside eat and sleep. Armadillos are **nocturnal** and tend to forage in the morning and early evening for beetles, termites and other insects and spend the rest of their time (up to 20 hours a day) in their burrow, not necessarily always fully asleep but certainly hard at rest.

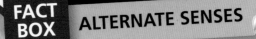

FACT BOX — **ALTERNATE SENSES**

Armadillos have poor eyesight but a keen sense of smell, which is what they rely on to find food and navigate their way around at night.

STINKIEST BIRD

HOATZIN

South America's swamps seem an appropriate home for the bizarre bird that's widely considered to be the stinkiest – the hoatzin. This bird seems to be a relic species with a lot of peculiar features, and scientists have long been baffled about which other living species are its closest relatives. Hoatzins are herbivores that use bacteria in part of their gut to ferment and help digest the fruit and leaves they eat. Although cattle do a similar thing, it's not seen in any other birds. Unfortunately, the fermentation process and types of leaves hoatzins consume give them a very unpleasant smell of manure!

FAST FACT

Sole survivor
Recent genetic research suggests the hoatzin is the only surviving member of a bird group that branched off on its own, just after the extinction of the dinosaurs.

LARGEST TORTOISE

GALÁPAGOS TORTOISE

This, the largest living tortoise species, is also one of the slowest-moving animals for its size. It can usually only make a top speed of just 1.6kph. Males, however, can seem more 'enthusiastic' during the mating season, when they've been tracked travelling as far as 13km in only two days on treks in search of females. Galápagos tortoises can reach a weight of more than 250kg with a shell longer than about 1.5m.

FAST FACT

Long lives
Galápagos tortoises are among the longest living vertebrates, with a lifespan known to extend for at least 150 years.

250kg

STRONGEST BITE FORCE

BLACK PIRANHA

For its body size, the black piranha has the most powerful bite of any carnivorous fish. It achieves this by having jaw muscles of an extraordinary size for its overall bodyweight, as well as having a highly specialised jaw-closing mechanism. This has resulted in a bite force that is equivalent to 30 times its bodyweight; three times more than the bite force that could be exerted by an American alligator if it were the same size.

UNIQUE FATHERLY CARE

FROG ACTORS

A Darwin's frog will roll onto its back and act dead when it is threatened.

DARWIN'S FROG

There is a range of ways animal fathers get involved in the birth or care of their offspring. But the strategy taken by male Darwin's frogs is one of the most bizarre. After the female lays her eggs in leaf litter, the male fertilises them and guards them for up to four weeks until tadpoles can be seen wriggling inside the eggs. The male then ingests the eggs and holds them in his vocal sac where they hatch a few days later. He keeps the developing tadpoles in his mouth until they change into tiny frogs and hop out of his mouth.

Glossary

Anaphylaxis — An extreme and sometimes deadly allergic reaction.

Bioluminescent — Describes the emission of light by a living organism.

Camouflaged — Hidden within the surrounding environment.

Decibel (dB) — A unit of measurement for the intensity of sound.

Genus — A group of closely related species.

Hibernating — Spending winter in a safe place.

Metabolism — The chemical processes going on inside organisms to maintain life.

Migration — Travel from one place to another.

Nocturnal — Active at night.

Plankton — Tiny organisms floating in fresh or sea water.

Predator — An animal that hunts and eats other animals.

Satellite tags — Devices that track animals by sending information about their movements to satellites.

Savannah — A grassy tropical or subtropical plain.

Supercolony — Massive groups of animals living closely with each other.

Terrestrial — Living on land.

FURTHER READING

Australia's Most Extreme
2015, Australian Geographic

Mythical Monsters
2015, Australian Geographic

The Concise Animal Encyclopedia
2013, Australian Geographic

Children's Animal Atlas
2015, Australian Geographic